YOUR SEXUAL HEALTH™

SYPHILIS

PHILIP WOLNY

ROSEN
PUBLISHING®

New York

Published in 2016 by The Rosen Publishing Group, Inc.
29 East 21st Street, New York, NY 10010

Copyright © 2016 by The Rosen Publishing Group, Inc.

First Edition

Library of Congress Cataloging-in-Publication Data

Wolny, Philip.
Syphilis/Philip Wolny.—First edition.
    pages cm.—(Your sexual health)
Includes bibliographical references and index.
ISBN 978-1-4994-6062-9 (library bound)—ISBN 978-1-4994-6063-6 (pbk.)—
ISBN 978-1-4994-6064-3 (6-pack)
1. Syphilis—Popular works. I. Title.
RC201.W77 2016
616.95'13—dc23

                                                                    2014042690

Manufactured in the United States of America

CONTENTS

Good health is one of the greatest benefits of youth. As they mature, teens experiment with their sexuality in different ways. Doing so, they expose themselves and their young bodies to new risks. Among the most common health dangers facing teens is the possibility of contracting a sexually transmitted disease (STD), sometimes known as a sexually transmitted infection (STI). Any kind of sexual contact—whether oral, vaginal, or anal, straight or gay—may expose you to infections that affect you for years to come and may even threaten your life.

One of the less common STDs, syphilis is also one of the more dangerous ones. It can easily be mistaken for other, unrelated health problems. Left untreated, it can cause irreparable physical harm and, in the long-term, a miserable death.

Before modern medicine, syphilis was a much more feared disease that claimed millions of lives. Nowadays, there are effective treatments for this infection, especially at its earliest stages. That is why it pays to muster the courage to confront a possible infection head-on and not ignore it, hoping it goes away. Sufferers owe it to themselves and their own well-being. They also owe it to any past, current, or future sexual partners. The person from whom they caught the STD may not know he or she is infected, and the same might be the case for others unknowingly exposed to the infection.

Both long-term and new relationships can be complicated by STDs like syphilis. Knowledge, honesty, and positivity can arm sufferers against the effects of these infections.

STDs, including syphilis, do not only cause physical symptoms and suffering. They can also be a cause of social stigma. Infections may cause teens embarrassment and shame, making them hide their infections, even from those they trust. They may fear that friends, family, and even their significant others or sexual partners will react badly to this news—for example, by rejecting, excluding, or even bullying them.

Finding out you have syphilis can be shocking and dispiriting. You may not know whom to turn to. That makes it that much more important not to face this challenge alone. The resources are out there to help young people especially. State, federal, and local programs provide cheap or free testing, counseling, and treatment, much of it anonymous and discrete. Support groups made up of others who have caught syphilis or other STDs can also be a huge help. In addition, a personal health crisis is exactly the time to use those personal resources many of us count on. Most teens have support networks they can leverage, including best friends, classmates, brothers or sisters, parents, guardians, or even grandparents.

However, the greatest cure, as with all STDs, is prevention. By learning how to effectively protect yourself against syphilis, you stand a good chance of never suffering from this sometimes misunderstood and insidious bacterial infection. Remember, knowledge is power. Understanding how to prevent, diagnose, treat, and cope with syphilis will help you maintain your sexual health. This knowledge will help you beat syphilis, or even avoid it altogether.

CHAPTER ONE

What Is Syphilis?

Syphilis is an infectious disease caused by a bacterium called *Treponema pallidum.* Bacteria are microorganisms, tiny living things existing in every part of the environment, many of them on human bodies and within them, too. They can be seen only with instruments that magnify their appearance thousands of times, such as microscopes.

Bacteria can be harmful, beneficial, or even neutral within the human body. Beneficial ones help the body's natural processes. Harmful ones attack the body's tissues and cause various complications. Many lead to major health problems, and even death. *Treponema pallidum* is a spirochete—a long, thin, coiled bacterium. It can harm several organ systems, and it can be fatal if left unchecked.

A HISTORICAL SCOURGE

Syphilis has probably existed for thousands of years, but its origins and exact movements

Artist Albrecht Dürer's fifteenth-century engraving *Syphilitic Man* depicts a sufferer of the disease.

among human populations remain uncertain. One theory is that it originated in the New World and was brought back to Europe by explorers. Other scientists think that syphilis has existed in both the Eastern and Western Hemispheres for millennia. Some of its symptoms among Europeans may have been confused with those of leprosy, which has similar effects as late-stage syphilis.

Syphilis really became widespread in Europe only around the sixteenth century. Because it was so little understood during a time when medical knowledge was far more primitive, its late-stage symptoms were even more devastating to sufferers then. Syphilis thus gained its fearsome reputation.

It was only in modern times that this notorious illness was significantly curbed, at least in developed nations. In the United States, syphilis cases hit a peak of about 106,000 in 1947, according

In the highly controversial and unethical Tuskegee syphilis experiment that ran from 1932 to 1972, the U.S. Health Service intentionally infected poor African American farmers in Alabama with syphilis to study the disease. The farmers believed they were merely receiving free health care.

to the U.S. Centers for Disease Control and Prevention (CDC). The widespread use of penicillin then helped reduce its spread greatly. Scientists declared the disease almost eradicated in North America around 2000, but it has since rebounded. Meanwhile, in the developing world, millions are infected annually.

THE WONDER DRUG

Before the twentieth century, thousands of people died annually when their syphilis infections were treated with toxic substances, including ones like mercury and arsenic. The antibiotic penicillin had few comparable side effects. Along with syphilis, it fought dozens of other ailments, earning the nickname "the wonder drug."

In 1943, doctors at the U.S. Marine Hospital on Staten Island, New York, cured four patients of syphilis within eight days. This was a huge boon for the military at the height of hostilities. Prior to that, syphilis, gonorrhea, and other STDs took many soldiers out of commission for as long as months at a time. The military even printed thousands of posters warning of the dangers of these STDs. The need to produce large amounts of penicillin quickly to give to many thousands of troops would translate to mass-producing it for civilian uses after the war, too.

TRANSMISSION

Syphilis belongs to a class of diseases called STDs: sexually transmitted diseases. While it can occasionally be acquired by nonsexual means, such transmission of syphilis is uncommon. For example, cases where someone has gotten the disease from kissing an infected person are not entirely unheard of, but they are still rare. This requires actual contact with an active sore on or in the infected person's mouth and an abrasion or cut on the other person.

The *Treponema pallidum* bacterium needs moisture to survive and thrive. That is why its main mode of transmission between individuals is through sexual contact. Another way it spreads is from an infected pregnant mother to her unborn child. Intravenous (IV) drug users could also potentially catch syphilis by sharing needles, but this method of transmission is relatively low and not as risky as sexual contact.

Syphilis is not spread through casual contact. You cannot get it by sharing a meal or a drink with someone, or by using the same utensils. Nor does the bacterium survive in bathtubs or showers, pools, or toilets. It is not airborne, like the viruses responsible for the common cold. You cannot transfer it to another person via a doorknob or by sharing clothing.

PREVENTION

There are ways to prevent the spread of syphilis, some more effective than others. Transmission is primarily through vaginal, oral, or anal sexual contact, and the most surefire preventative method is to avoid these activities altogether.

Barring abstinence, the next best thing is to limit your possible exposure. One way is by remaining in a monogamous relationship with an uninfected person, which means dating only

A healthy relationship includes honesty, even if it means revealing painful or uncomfortable facts, such as a syphilis infection.

one steady partner at a time. Each person in the relationship should commit to the other. Those who change partners often, or maintain several sexual relationships at once, tend to significantly increase their chances of catching not only syphilis but other STDs as well, such as HPV, chlamydia, gonorrhea, or even HIV.

EQUAL OPPORTUNITY INFECTIOUS AGENT

Like other STDs, syphilis does not discriminate. Whatever your sexual orientation, ethnicity, or social class is, syphilis can harm you. Inaccurate perceptions of who is prone to syphilis, and who is not, only serve to give people a false—and dangerous—sense of security in the face of this serious disease. If someone tells you that "only those kind of people" contract syphilis, it is about as accurate as the myth that you cannot catch certain STDs or become pregnant if you take a shower after sex—in other words, it's dead wrong.

MINIMIZING RISK

While syphilis will not infect any particular kind of person more readily than another, there are lifestyle and behavior choices that can put you at greater risk of being infected— with syphilis and a host of other STDs, both viral and bacterial.

Having multiple sexual partners in a short span of time, or dating several partners at once, puts someone at greater risk of syphilis exposure. Other behaviors can indirectly put you in situations that make you more vulnerable. For example, underage binge drinking and substance abuse can impair a young person's judgment in deciding with whom or when to engage in sexual behavior.

Those who engage in such behaviors tend to catch syphilis and other STDs at greater rates. *Science Daily* reported in September 2008 how a Johns Hopkins University School of Medicine study noted a link between binge drinking and risky behaviors among young women. Women had a higher chance of impairment, but both men and women are more likely to engage in unsafe sex when intoxicated and to choose to go ahead with it in situations that they would have avoided if sober.

Teens who have already contracted syphilis need to remember that the disease can increase a person's vulnerability to other diseases. Syphilitic sores are entry points for other infections, including HIV. The presence of syphilis may also signal the presence of other STDs, since these infections tend to cluster in patients. You should test for as many other types of STDs as you can if you have screened positive for syphilis.

CONDOMS

Regardless of with whom you are intimate, one of the most important defenses against syphilis is using a condom. A latex condom is the most effective barrier for preventing the transfer of bacteria from active sores to a victim. The female condom, which is a latex pouch that is put into the vagina, performs a similar function.

However, even a condom is not 100 percent guaranteed to protect against syphilis transmission. Condoms can significantly reduce the risk, but if certain infected areas are exposed and come in contact with one's partner, then syphilis can be spread. Sexually active people must be ever vigilant. Condoms may break or tear without either partner even noticing.

CHAPTER TWO

Diagnosing Syphilis

The main symptom of a syphilis infection when it is first spread, called primary syphilis, is a sore called a chancre. Chancre sores occur at the point of contact where the infection first affects the person receiving it. Almost all of the time, they are painless, and sufferers may not even notice they have developed them. A chancre is an open sore that has a firm base.

In women, chancre sores can develop on the outside or inside of the vagina or in the cervix, directly above the vagina. Even prominent, exterior sores might not be immediately visible or noticeable. Sometimes, chancres might develop on the folds of the labia and thus remain inconspicuous.

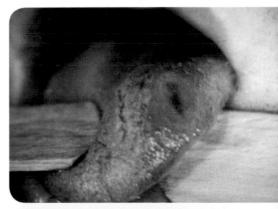

The primary chancre seen here is a sign of the first stage of syphilis.

Males contracting syphilis get chancres on the penis, anus, and rectum. These can remain unnoticed when developing in certain areas: in the folds of the foreskin of the penis, under the scrotum, or at the base of the penis.

In both sexes, chancre sores can occur on the mouth, lips, or tongue, and sometimes even on the hands or eyes. Exposure in this area of the body is most likely when someone engages in oral sex with an infected person with an active sore on the genitals.

CHANCRE, CANKER, OR HERPES?

One thing you may become confused about if you get a sore is what kind of infection is truly the cause. The chancre sores that accompany syphilis may occasionally look like other infections—specifically, the cold sores many people get because they carry the herpes simplex virus, or "canker" sores, which are themselves often incorrectly referred to as cold sores.

Cold sores can be irritating, even painful, as can canker sores. Both are relatively harmless. Meanwhile, the painless syphilis chancre inflammation can be anything but. You might go months or even years without detection.

Syphilis has been and is still often mistaken for other ailments including herpes, measles, typhus, smallpox, fungal infections, leprosy, and dozens of other infections, as well as for and everyday phenomena, such as ingrown hairs, acne, and minor injuries. Consequently, it has sometimes been known as "the great imitator." It can be overlooked because, unlike bacterial infections like gonorrhea, there is no burning or discharge.

DO I HAVE SYPHILIS?

You may have discovered a mysterious sore on your body and suspect it is syphilis. Or you may not exhibit any known symptoms and yet be sexually active. As with other STDs, it takes only one time to get infected. And it does not matter whether it was "just" oral sex or any other kind of activity. One particular kind of sexual activity is rarely safer than another when one's partner has active, and hence contagious, sores.

Even if your partner has been tested very recently, and you trust absolutely that he or she has been monogamous, any sexual activity carries a risk with it. Despite everything you thought you or your partner have done properly, you can catch still syphilis. But how do you really know for sure if you have it?

FINDING OUT FOR SURE

The most surefire way to uncover syphilis is to get tested at a doctor's office or a health clinic specializing in STD screenings and treatment.

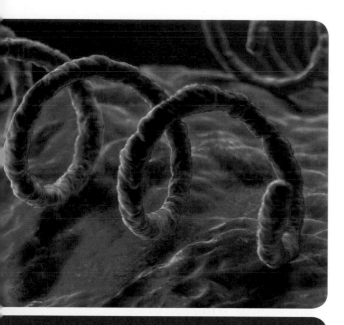

This 3D visualization of the microscopic *Treponema pallidum*, the bacterium behind syphilis, shows its curled structure.

There are several pros and cons as to which course might be best.

You may feel comfortable with a doctor you already know and trust. On the other hand, your doctor may be a family friend with whom you are not comfortable discussing your sexual health. It is also possible that your primary care doctor does not provide the necessary tests, or that the cost of these tests might be more expensive through your family practitioner.

A better option might be to choose getting tested at an STD clinic. The benefits are cheaper, and usually anonymous, testing, especially if your state, county, or locality funds low-income health services. Many organizations also offer counseling geared especially at adolescents and young people. Another group that offers similar services is Planned Parenthood.

Consult the Internet or other listings for the closest local resources. Those offering both screening and treatment are best. Make sure to plan accordingly: low-cost or free clinics might have irregular hours or long waits for their affordable care.

THE TEST FOR SYPHILIS

Some people avoid getting tested for syphilis. They believe "what I don't know can't hurt me." Others may simply be nervous about the testing itself. They think it might be painful, uncomfortable, or embarrassing. The slight social discomfort of requesting a syphilis screening, or the minor physical discomfort of getting a drop of blood taken, however, are little compared to the risk of a painful and destructive condition taking your health—even your life—in the years to come. In this case, what you don't know can hurt you—badly.

Diagnosing syphilis requires two steps. The first is meant to detect that a syphilis infection

DARKFIELD MICROSCOPY AND MOLECULAR TESTING

Other tests are less common but test directly for syphilis itself. These include darkfield microscopy, in which a chancre sore is scraped and then the samples are placed on a slide and viewed through a microscope. Molecular testing is another process used to confirm the presence of syphilis. It looks for genetic material of the bacteria from a blood or spinal fluid sample.

is a definite possibility. If the first step results in a positive, then the second step is a more specific diagnostic test. The initial step does not test directly for syphilis. Instead, it tests for syphilis antibodies in the blood. Antibodies are protein molecules the body creates to fight diseases, including infections caused by bacteria and viruses. The human body makes antibodies that respond to syphilis, but similar ones also arise when someone has Lyme disease, certain kinds of pneumonia, malaria, and other conditions, like tuberculosis and lupus. This type of screening is nontreponemal, since it may also result in false-positives for patients in any of those categories. The two kinds of nontreponemal screening are rapid plasma reagin (RPR), a rapid diagnostic test (any test that provides a result in twenty minutes to a couple of hours) and the Venereal Disease Research Laboratory (VDRL) test. These are both blood tests that require the extraction of a small blood sample.

A second set of tests further confirms a syphilis infection. These treponemal tests are less likely to turn up false-positives because of other conditions a person has. They do have one weakness, though. They test only whether someone has at some point been infected. This means they will still yield false-positives if the person being tested has been cured of syphilis.

MYTHS AND FACTS

MYTH
If you catch syphilis, you can expect a miserable and slow decline in your health.

FACT
Syphilis is completely curable in its early stages and treatable in its later ones, which most people never even experience.

MYTH
Syphilis affects only those who are sexually promiscuous.

FACT
It takes only a single time to expose oneself to syphilis.

MYTH
You can always tell from visual clues whether someone has syphilis.

FACT
Only the rare advanced cases of syphilis exhibit easily noticed visible symptoms. Chancres are not always present, and when they are, they tend to be on concealed parts of the body.

CHAPTER THREE

The Four Stages of Syphilis

Syphilis will develop through four main stages, assuming that it is not treated and cured quickly. The first, or primary, stage of syphilis is marked by the appearance of one or more of the chancre sores mentioned earlier. Each open, reddish sore is painless, round or oval, and firm. It is relatively clean, with no pus or discharge. It can be easily overlooked. If you get one, it will typically appear as early as two weeks or as late as ten or more weeks after exposure. These lesions, without being treated, typically go away within about a month and a half.

Another symptom affects the lymph nodes (oval-shaped organs that are part of the human immune system) in the groin and inner thighs. These may swell and harden, and become tender.

SECONDARY SYPHILIS

The next stage, secondary syphilis, marks a more serious escalation for many syphilis

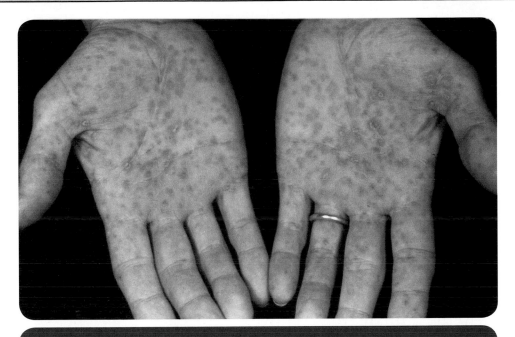

Shown here are the palms of a syphilis sufferer, demonstrating the rash that may occur during the secondary stage of syphilis.

patients. The bacterial infection travels through your blood, entering your skin cells, liver, and joints. It also affects the lymphatic system, the muscles, and the brain.

When the chancres from the first stage have healed, they are often followed by a rash that arises about six weeks later or as late as three months after. These rashes most commonly occur on the palms or the soles of the feet. Usually, the rash doesn't itch, as some rashes tend to. At the same time, chancres may develop in one's mouth or throat and even deeper within the body, on one's bones and internal organs.

During the secondary stage, syphilis can be extremely contagious. Bacteria secrete from the chancres and can easily spread, especially through sexual activity. Other symptoms might cause some real discomfort: sufferers might get sore throats or headaches, develop a fever, or experience aches and joint pains. Some people even lose some of their hair.

As reported on Healthcommunities.com, a "significant number of patients do not develop symptoms at this stage of the disease." This may seem like a blessing, but it can end up being a mixed one. Those who never experience symptoms may never know they have syphilis and thus never seek the needed treatment. The symptoms of secondary syphilis could subside and disappear in a couple of weeks. Others have these symptoms recur over the course of months, even a year.

THE LATENT STAGE

When the symptoms of secondary syphilis go away, and assuming the infection is not treated at even this late stage, a carrier can enter a time during which no symptoms occur. This is called the latent stage, or latency. Latent means "hidden" or "concealed." This does not mean that symptoms will not return, however. Many researchers do not consider this a true stage of the disease, since there are no symptoms. Meanwhile, *Treponema pallidum* hides out in the body.

Some people's latent stage lasts perhaps one to three years. Other carriers may have twenty or even thirty years without symptoms. A high percentage—about 70 percent or more—of syphilis carriers who remain untreated actually never get

Many carriers of syphilis experience latency, during which they might forget they have the infection at all, even for years at a time.

sick again. The sooner latency ends, the more manageable syphilis tends to be. For example, someone whose syphilis returns within a few months after the secondary stage ends stands a much better chance of surviving.

TERTIARY SYPHILIS

If syphilis comes back after latency, it is called tertiary syphilis, or late syphilis. This stage presents the most advanced, frightening, and dangerous potential health problems. The patient will likely not be contagious anymore, but that is probably the sole consolation. *Treponema pallidum* reactivates and begins to multiply. Syphilis begins to spread through much of the body. The bones and joints are affected, as well as the eyes. Blindness is a common symptom of this late stage. Even more important, organ systems are imperiled.

GUMMATOUS DISEASE

Sufferers of later-stage syphilis can develop gummas. These are tumors or large growths (granulomas) that are nonmalignant (non-cancerous) but can be large and rubbery. These are actually a reaction of the human immune system in a last-ditch effort to fight off syphilis. In this case, the tissues grow to block or slow down the progress of the bacteria.

They can occur anywhere in the body, both internally and at the surface of the skin. Syphilitic gummas commonly affect a person's joints when they grow on the skeleton. They often form on the leg, below the knee. When they grow inside the body—for example, on the liver—they may affect organ functions. Other effects are bone and joint pain from the inflammation. Gummas appear, on average, at around fifteen years after syphilis infection but can develop far sooner, and sometimes decades later.

SYPHILIS AND THE CARDIOVASCULAR SYSTEM

One of systems harmed by tertiary syphilis is the cardiovascular system, including the blood vessels and main arteries. Syphilis causes narrowing of the blood vessels. This may lead to chest pain and may eventually help cause a heart attack, possibly a fatal one.

The most important artery leading from the heart to the abdomen, the aorta, is also affected. The muscular and elastic tissue that helps pump blood in the body becomes inflamed. This inflammation weakens that tissue, leaving it less able to do its job. The same is true for the heart valves that open and close to pump blood. Failure of the heart valves leads to heart failure and death. A weakened aorta can lead to a heart murmur. It can even rupture, an event called an aortic aneurysm, which can kill the patient.

NEUROSYPHILIS

Neurosyphilis occurs when the disease causes deterioration of the human nervous system, especially the brain and spinal cord. While relatively rare, it remains a possibility for those leaving syphilis untreated. There are several categories of neurosyphilis, which depend on the severity and extent of the infection. It mostly afflicts those in the tertiary stage. As the CDC

While uncommon, later stages of the disease can cause great damage. The human skull displayed here was ravaged by a case of neurosyphilis.

warns, however, it can occur at any stage of syphilis infection.

GENERAL PARESIS

Another possible outcome is general paresis. This can be confused with other mental disorders and may include noticeable mental impairment. The person may seem "off" in some way, experiencing mood swings or sharp shifts in personality. Memory problems and disorientation can occur, as well as depression.

Advanced cases are marked by chronic dementia and even hallucinations. This is one reason that some people confuse it for Alzheimer's disease. General paresis takes around thirty years to arise. Penicillin is prescribed in treating it, but, as with the other late-stage syphilitic afflictions, the antibiotic can only beat back the infection; it cannot reverse the damage already done. It is rare these days in developed nations, but it was a fearsome and widespread condition in the distant past, when it was known as "general paresis of the insane."

MENINGOVASCULAR NEUROSYPHILIS

Meningovascular neurosyphilis—sometimes known as meningeal neurosyphilis—generally occurs in the late stage, though it can also develop in someone who has recently been infected, either within the first few months or within years of exposure. Nausea, vomiting, a stiff neck, and headaches are typical symptoms. Loss of vision and hearing can occur, too. Its name derives from the meninges, the membranes that cover the central nervous system, which it inflames, along with the small blood vessels in the brain itself.

TABES DORSALIS

Tabes dorsalis, also known as syphilitic myelopathy, is another neurological manifestation of syphilis, and it is more common in males than females. In Latin, *tabes* means "shriveling" or "decay," while *dorsalis* refers to the back. Syphilis damages the nerves in the spinal cord, which compromises the sensory signals a person receives from the surrounding world. The earliest symptoms are sharp and sudden pains in the legs, which can repeat several times a day for days on end. Other signs are a sense of tingling, burning, or coldness in the lower regions.

This particular complication of syphilis brings with it poor balance and coordination, which can cause trouble with walking and other common movements. Called sensory ataxia, this condition comes from being unable to judge one's position in relation to the ground. People with ataxia find it hard to walk in a straight line or over uneven surfaces. They also have difficulty navigating sudden turns.

Victims' feet may become less sensitive to stimuli and temperature changes, becoming numb. Ulcers may also develop on the feet. Other effects of tabes dorsalis that are nerve-related are problems with vision, hearing, and a loss of control of bladder and bowel movements.

CHAPTER FOUR

Treating Syphilis

I f you have been or plan to be sexually active, avoiding syphilis and other STDs is part of the territory. If you catch it and discover your infection early on, the resources are out there to help you overcome syphilis and have a complete recovery. However, this means getting treatment as soon as you can.

PENICILLIN: BEATING BACK SYPHILIS

The first and best treatment for syphilis during the first stage is antibiotics. By far, the most common treatment for syphilis is the antibiotic penicillin. Also used for other bacterial conditions, like ear infections, a single dose of penicillin often cures syphilis if the infection has occurred within the last year. The type used for syphilis is Benzylpenicillin, or penicillin G, which is also used for pneumonia, meningitis, and other ailments.

Penicillin cures syphilis in the primary stage. It is administered either with a shot, often

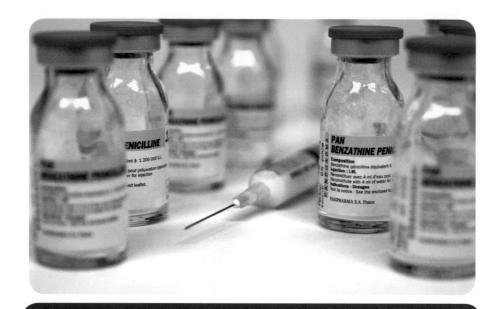

Syphilis is treated primarily with penicillin. In many cases, penicillin is administered to patients using syringes.

injected directly into the muscles of the buttocks (intramuscularly) or provided intravenously—that is, through a needle into the bloodstream. Unlike other antibiotics, unfortunately, penicillin does not seem to be effective when taken orally, in pill form.

Patients allergic to penicillin must be extra careful. This allergy is an overreaction of one's immune system to the antibiotic entering the body. Some people have mild reactions. Common symptoms of this allergy include rashes, hives, itchy eyes, and swelling in the face, on the tongue, or in and around the mouth.

A more severe reaction called anaphylaxis can occur, often as quickly as an hour after taking penicillin. The victim's bodily tissues tighten up, and the resulting effects include difficulty breathing, wheezing, dizziness and loss of consciousness, a quickened or weakened pulse, the skin turning blue, and gastrointestinal reactions like nausea, diarrhea, and vomiting.

Doctors will first try to desensitize an allergic patient to penicillin slowly, especially if they feel that the symptoms are minor compared to the effectiveness of penicillin as a syphilis cure. Severe allergies prevent easy desensitization, so alternative antibiotics may be prescribed, such as doxycycline, tetracycline, ceftriaxone, or azithromycin. These have been shown to be adequate for the first and second stages. But nothing quite substitutes for penicillin in a late-stage patient.

After treatment, doctors will usually require that you come in for at least two follow-up blood tests, within six months and a year after your initial treatment. This is to make sure that the treatment has been effective and that the syphilis has not bounced back.

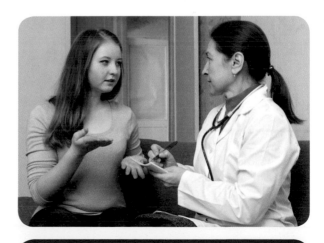

Doctors are trained and experienced in helping young people obtain and get through syphilis treatment smoothly.

A SYPHILIS VACCINE?

There is currently no vaccine for syphilis. Luckily, penicillin has had staying power

 THE JARISCH-HERXHEIMER REACTION

Penicillin kills *Treponema pallidum*, but it does not always do so without some cost. How your body reacts to penicillin, even if you are not allergic, will differ from others' reactions. Every person's experience with treatment is different. Many suffer from what is known as the Jarisch-Herxheimer reaction. This is your body's response to the toxins released when bacteria are killed inside you. Within several hours of first administering antibiotics, you may experience any or all of the following symptoms: a rash, or rashes; joint and muscle aches and/or pains; headaches; chills; and a high fever. Do not be concerned, however, since these are common reactions. They usually clear up in a day or so. Always mention any complications or lingering side effects to your doctor or clinician, just to be safe.

when it comes to fighting this disease. Other bacterial STDs, like gonorrhea, have developed strains in recent years with increased resistance to antibiotics. Ever-more resistant strains might demand larger doses, although it is a delicate balancing act because using antibiotics carelessly can cause unexpectedly strong, newer strains of diseases to arise in human populations. The continuing effectiveness of penicillin has not made creating a syphilis vaccine a top priority for the medical field.

LATER-STAGE TREATMENTS

The earlier you catch a syphilis infection, the less penicillin you will need to treat it. Early enough, just one penicillin injection may do the trick and kill off all the bacteria in your body. A single injection is usually recommended for most patients with primary, secondary, or early latent syphilis.

Patients with late latent syphilis or tertiary syphilis, if they are not suffering from neurosyphilis, are treated with one dose a week of penicillin, lasting three weeks. Still others, further down the road into tertiary syphilis, especially neurosyphilis, need more penicillin. This is because they have more of the syphilis-causing bacteria in their bodies and probably in a variety of organ systems. The recommended treatment for both symptomatic and asymptomatic carriers is a dose of the antibiotic once every four hours for ten to fourteen days. An alternative treatment is daily injections once a day with procaine benzylpenicillin, a mix of penicillin and the anesthetic (painkiller) procaine.

Other antibiotics, such as ceftriaxone, may be attempted if someone is truly allergic and has a more serious late-stage form of syphilis. Unfortunately, penicillin is still the only truly effective treatment for nuerosyphilis and other late-stage syphilitic ailments.

SYPHILIS AND HIV

Syphilis alone can be a handful to deal with if left unchecked within your body. With HIV (human immunodeficiency virus), the dangers dramatically increase. Syphilis itself can increase the chances of catching HIV. That is because active sores act as open doors for HIV. The CDC estimates that someone having sexual contact with an HIV-infected person has at least two to as many as fives times a greater risk of contracting HIV when syphilis is present.

Once infected, carrying both at the same time is even more dangerous. HIV the cause of AIDS, is still deadly and widespread. Even effective treatments in recent years have not curbed its deadly effects in many patients.

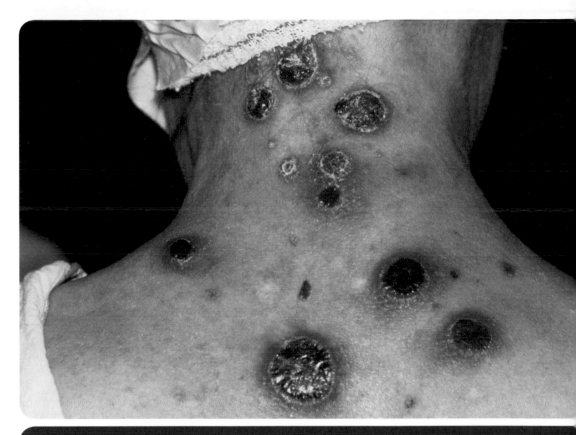

Shown here is another possible symptom of secondary syphilis: rash and inflammations that have flared up on a victim's neck and back.

The HIV/syphilis combination is so perilous because while syphilis may or may not advance through to the tertiary stage on its own, HIV ravages the immune system so badly that syphilis often does far worse damage than it ordinarily would. In many cases, HIV speeds up the spread of syphilis throughout the body.

10 GREAT QUESTIONS
TO ASK A DOCTOR ABOUT SYPHILIS

1. How contagious is syphilis compared to other STDs?

2. Are scientists working on a vaccine for syphilis?

3. Is there any way to distinguish syphilis chancre sores from those of other STDs?

4. How effective is penicillin in treating a new case of syphilis?

5. What are the general side effects of penicillin and other treatments?

6. Should I be concerned more by syphilis if I have any chronic medical condition?

7. How much damage has syphilis already to done to me, if any?

8. Will my body bounce back from what syphilis has already done?

9. How much does syphilis treatment cost, including penicillin and other drugs?

10. How long do the secondary stage symptoms of syphilis stick around?

CHAPTER FIVE

Dealing with Syphilis

I t can take time for the shock of a syphilis diagnosis to register. Some people may be getting test results back because they did notice symptoms and are thus somewhat better prepared. A teen undergoing routine screening may have a harder time dealing with this unwelcome surprise than someone with symptoms. For anybody, it can be demoralizing and hard to internalize, or accept, a positive diagnosis.

FULL DISCLOSURE

If you are in a relationship, revealing your infection to your partner is one of the most important steps you will take. It may be hard to summon up the courage. You may still be reeling from the news, after all.

Nevertheless, you owe it to yourself, him or her, and other sexual partners you have had to be honest and straightforward about your

In a world of texting and social media, talking about a syphilis infection face-to-face is the best and most discreet way to face the problem together.

condition. It may be uncomfortable and embarrassing. You might be worried about angering or alienating your partner. But you will be saving him or her from much grief in the future. With syphilis, an ounce of prevention really is worth a pound of cure.

COVERING ALL BASES

A common observation when it comes to the spread of STDs is that when you sleep with someone, in reality you are sleeping with everyone that person has slept with before, and vice versa. If doctors suspect that someone may have been exposed, they will highly recommend that all of his or her sexual partners get screened for syphilis. It is best to cover all bases and go back at least three months before diagnosis.

It is important to talk to former partners about a diagnosis. Seeking out former partners can be tricky, but it needs to be done. It will be

TALKING TO YOUR PARTNER ABOUT SYPHILIS

In cases where the trail of syphilis infection is uncertain (whether your partner gave it to you, or vice versa), it is important to be compassionate and patient and not sound like you are attacking someone by bringing up this uncomfortable issue.

You may also just be starting out a relationship. Tell a new partner as soon as it seems that things might get intimate. Someone with an active flare-up, especially early syphilis, may want to avoid even kissing someone because an open sore inside the mouth could be dangerous. The worst time to bring something up is right before engaging in sexual activity. The person may feel pressured to do something with you or reject you because he or she feels lied to.

Another question is whether to be direct or indirect in your approach. Knowing a partner's personality (and yourself) will help you decide the best way for you to reveal your secret. You could begin the conversation with a simple, "Let's talk about protection and STDs," and then work from there. Another way is to simply launch into it.

Be prepared for possible concern from your partner. Arm yourself with knowledge about how syphilis is, and isn't, spread. This will reassure the person that you know what you are doing, and your confidence and honesty will shine through. Often, having this conversation may show you how much a potential partner cares about you. You may be pleasantly surprised: a quality partner will be open-minded and willing to work with you.

easier or harder depending on the number of partners you have been involved with. It is never easy to make that call to someone, especially to an ex—someone whom you may not communicate or be on good terms with anymore. Doing it more than once may emotionally drain you. However, it should get easier with time. You will hopefully experience a sense of relief and well-being from coming clean.

WHAT WILL PEOPLE THINK?

One reason you may be anxious about confiding in anyone else about your syphilis diagnosis is the potential fallout from people finding out. You may rightfully be wary of your privacy being violated and your reputation attacked on social networks.

　　The last thing you want or need is for your sexual health to be the subject of the whole school's Twitter or Facebook updates. This anxiety might make you think twice about seeking help or confiding in someone for the emotional support you will need. At some point, you have seen someone's name being dragged through the mud due to something he or she may or may not have done or because of a rumor about his or her behavior. It may even have involved a story about someone with an STD. Few things are more hurtful than being ganged up on in this way.

　　But it is necessary to get past this, too. A diagnosis of syphilis is just the kind of crisis

While you might be most reluctant to tell an adult, such as a family member or close family friend, about your syphilis diagnosis, those with experience may have the wisdom and patience you need to help you get through a trying time.

in which you truly need your personal support network to be there for you. Choose wisely, and tell only the people you absolutely feel you have to. You will need every bit of help to get through the confusion, shame, discomfort, and anxiety a syphilis diagnosis brings with it.

Ultimately, remember that you are not alone out there. According to the CDC, as reported in *Forbes* magazine in May 2014, syphilis cases nearly doubled from 2012 to 2013, from 8,724 to 16,663. Remember, too, that these are only cases that were reported.

DEALING WITH SHAME

A natural reaction, and one that many people have when they find out they have caught syphilis, is feelings of shame. Sex is often an awkward, or even taboo, topic of discussion to begin with, especially between young people and parents or other adults in authority. This embarrassment and silence surrounding sex extends to STDs like syphilis. A herpes sore on the mouth may be considered normal, with 80 percent of Americans carrying HSV-1, or oral herpes, while a syphilis chancre is something few would volunteer to discuss.

At the same time, a syphilis diagnosis is something a young person takes very personally. Infected teens may think it reflects badly on them as individuals, that they are somehow seen as immoral or promiscuous—dirty somehow—in the eyes of their peers and adults.

The stigma can be particularly hard on those who come from devout, religious backgrounds, but it stings for anybody. Knowing you have syphilis may make you beat yourself up and question yourself as a person. You may fear that no one else will want to have you as a partner, or even as a friend. It is easy to let syphilis define you.

Realizing that you are not defined by an infection may be difficult, but it is both necessary and do-able. The key is seeing it as an unfortunate accident, much like catching the common flu one day while out at the super-market. Contracting syphilis does not mean you were weak or careless, just unlucky.

Shame is not only counterproductive; it can be harmful, too. It is another way of blaming yourself. Of course, this is another dead end: we cannot change the past. All one can do is move on and try to do the right thing in the future.

NEGATIVE COPING TECHNIQUES

Beating yourself up over it will not help you get past syphilis. It just makes things worse. People who dwell on their shame in such situations tend to hide from their problems or engage in negative coping strategies. Some people slip into a depression, signs of which include simply withdrawing from social interaction and one's favorite activities. Negative coping strategies can also mean destructive behaviors, including self-harm and substance abuse. It depends whether one reacts to stress by withdrawing or lashing out. Neither will really help, in the short or long term. Having syphilis is bad enough, without piling extra problems on top of that.

Shame can also lead to hiding one's diagnosis, and consequently cutting off the necessary family, peer, and community connections necessary to get treatment and receive needed emotional or psychological counseling and support.

Rather than wallowing in shame, talking about it with a trusted adult or even a trained professional can help you sort through your feelings, come to terms with the shame you feel, and even dispel the anger you may have toward others due to your infection. There is no one-size-fits-all approach, but choosing

ONLINE SAFETY

Looking up reputable websites (like those of the CDC or National Institutes of Health, for example) is a good start when researching syphilis. The Internet can also help you find clinics and support. Online advice and information about syphilis should be approached with caution, however. Not all of it will be correct or properly vetted by professionals.

Be equally careful when it comes to online support groups, chat rooms, and hotlines. While some are helpful and perform an invaluable service–especially for those who want to vent anonymously–always protect your identity and your privacy. Distrust those who ask for money or make unusual requests. It is bad enough to have prey misfortune of contracting an STD without falling to Internet predators, con artists, identity thieves, or others seeking to take advantage of the vulnerable.

positivity will open more doors than denial and resentment.

THERAPY AND COUNSELING

A good idea for many young people who feel unsettled by their syphilis diagnosis is to seek counseling or therapy. Clinics, doctors, government health professionals, and even clergy may be able to refer you to someone in your area or to a counseling program that may be low-cost or even free. Help might be available one-on-one with a special counselor or in group settings.

Counseling or therapy can help you get over the emotional effects of your syphilis ordeal and can also help you express your feelings, set goals, and develop coping skills and stress-reduction techniques. Many people benefit from the structure and guidance that these kind of programs offer. It is sometimes easier to confide in a stranger who nevertheless can be a caring and impartial listener, and who provides good, unbiased advice. Going to therapy with a caring partner can be even more empowering and can strengthen an already positive relationship.

CHAPTER SIX

Beyond Syphilis: Coming to Terms and Looking Forward

Dealing with syphilis successfully means overcoming the disease and becoming a stronger person who has beaten back not just syphilis but all the negative fallout it can bring. Overcoming syphilis also means staying healthy, positive, and open-minded, and staying sympathetic to others who may experience a similar crisis.

REGULAR TESTING

Getting tested regularly is crucial, for those who have beat syphilis and for those who have never been diagnosed with an STD of any kind. Everyone who is sexually active should attempt to get screened at least once a year.

There is the temptation, of course, to become complacent in keeping this annual schedule. Anyone who falls into any of these categories especially should not miss their yearly screening: those who have tested positive for other STDs; those who have had sex of any kind with more than one partner since the last screening; users of intravenous drugs; men who have sex with men; women who are pregnant or planning on becoming pregnant; and victims of sexual assault.

Naturally, if you have been treated for syphilis, you must show up for regularly scheduled follow-up screenings. The first two are required, while follow-ups beyond those are highly recommended.

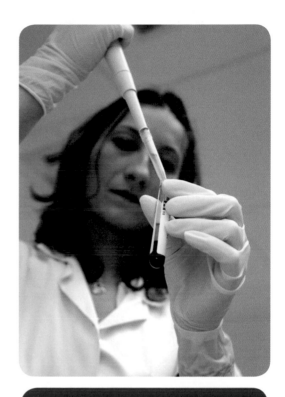

This medical professional is readying a pregnancy screening that will be accompanied by a syphilis screening.

DOWN THE ROAD: CONGENITAL SYPHILIS

For women who hope to someday be mothers, treating syphilis, or any STD, is particularly urgent. Syphilis can spread from a pregnant mother to a child in the womb, with possibly terrible results. The bacteria are usually transferred via the placenta, which connects the fetus to the uterus. If not earlier, getting a syphilis screening upon learning you are pregnant is crucial to protecting you and your baby. The National Institutes of Health estimate that 50 percent of children that contract syphilis before birth die in the womb or shortly after being born.

Newborns with congenital syphilis may

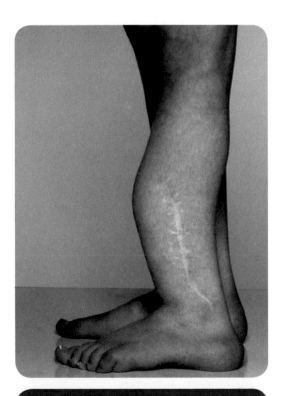

suffer from fever or unusual irritability, failure to gain weight or thrive (grow and develop properly), or rashes on the face, mouth, anus, and genitals. Infants sometimes suffer mucus, pus, and/or bloody discharge from the nose. These early symptoms are considered early congenital syphilis and manifest in the first three months of a child's life.

Other babies can get a physical deformity called "saddle nose"— they are missing the bridge of the nose most

Another possible effect of congenital syphilis is malformed bone structure.

people are born with. Fetuses that contract the disease early have a higher chance of being stillborn.

The majority of infected children are asymptomatic at birth but develop late congenital syphilis after about two years of life. Sadly, these very young children can experience similar symptoms to adults entering their tertiary stage of infection, like paresis and tabes.

They may also have their own unique symptoms. Among these are Hutchinson teeth, which have an unusual notched and pegged appearance. Other problems include eye disorders, impaired hearing or deafness, bone pain and malformed arms or legs, and gray patches and skin scarring in the groin area.

Infected women who receive penicillin treatment early in their pregnancy greatly reduce the chance of their baby developing congenital syphilis.

FROM ERADICATION TO COMEBACK

Many of the symptoms of syphilis—especially in its tertiary stage—are uncommon in developed western nations nowadays. They still exist in the developing world, where people do not have easy access to proper screening, treatment, or supplies.

The return of syphilis after many people thought it had been nearly defeated is a lesson all sexually active people should take to heart.

Dr. Monica Patton of the CDC announced in 2014, "After being on the verge of being eliminated in 2000 in the United States, syphilis cases have rebounded," according to *Forbes* magazine.

CDC statistics indicate that a vast majority of new cases (91 percent in 2013) were men. Gay and bisexual men, in particular, are testing positive more often. People with multiple partners in these groups, CDC officials have said, should get screened every three to six months.

NO ONE TO BLAME

People play the blame game with groups and on an individual level. Upon discovering you have contracted syphilis, you may become angry and blame another person for your misfortune–that is, the person you know or believe to have infected you.

This is a natural reaction, but part of coming to terms with your infection is realizing that there is no real guilty party. Most people pass syphilis to another person completely obliviously, since they themselves may not be aware of their infection. You have to remember that they, too, were likely exposed unknowingly. They are in the same boat as you. Getting over the urge to blame yourself will also help empower you to learn from the mistakes you have made, if any, and move on.

Another hard-hit demographic has been African Americans. The CDC says that black males are five times more likely than white males to get syphilis, while black women were thirteen times more likely than white women to contract it.

Despite a lower percentage of new female cases recently, women cannot let their guard down either. Women tend to experience milder symptoms than men and are thus more likely to mistake syphilis for something else or to remain asymptomatic.

It is wrong and inaccurate to blame any particular group of people for syphilis. The only things that control one's exposure to *Treponema pallidum* are the decisions on whether or not to have sex and whether to use condoms for

Among any random grouping of young people at a high school or on a college campus, it is entirely possible that someone in that group has, will have, or has had syphilis.

protection. Educators, medical professionals, and others all hope that, in the future, the stigma of syphilis becomes a thing of the past.

LOOKING ON THE BRIGHT SIDE

Remember, the frightening symptoms of late-stage syphilis happen to a very small minority of those who are infected. This potentially fatal infection is also among the most treatable STDs. If you catch it early enough, you will minimize your suffering and can live out your life without having to worry about it again. But it all starts with you deciding to get screened regularly, to take serious measures to prevent infection, and to make clear that others in your life should take the same precautions if they respect and love you.

Getting syphilis, rather than being a source of shame and a reason to withdraw from life, can serve as a wake-up call to reevaluate and change risky behavior. This can help someone who has recovered from getting reinfected with syphilis or contracting another STD. The strength you show in facing your problem head-on and doing right by the people around you, including those with whom you are intimate, can be a source of pride and empowerment that counters the shame that all too many sufferers of syphilis face.

GLOSSARY

asymptomatic Having an infection but showing none of the common symptoms of that infection.

cervix The constricted lower end of the female uterus, located above the vagina.

chancre The initial sore that appears with primary syphilis.

darkfield miscroscopy The use of microscopes that shine a light on the object being magnified and show it against a dark background.

intramuscular Refers to injections that are administered into a patient's muscle(s).

intravenous Relating to putting something into a patient's veins.

Jarisch-Herxheimer reaction A set of flulike, temporary reactions to penicillin treatments, particularly those for syphilis.

latency A period in an infection's life cyle in which it appears to have disappeared and during which a patient exhibits no symptoms.

nontreponemal Refers to initial screening that indicates a likelihood of syphilis.

spirochete A type of long and slender bacterium with a coiled structure.

tabes dorsalis A particular set of symptoms of late syphilis caused by the nerves in the victim's spinal cord being damaged.

tertiary The third stage or item in a series of multiple items.

treponemal Refers to secondary blood tests that confirm the presence of syphilis.

FOR MORE INFORMATION

Advocates for Youth
2000 M Street NW, Suite 750
Washington, DC 20036
(202) 419-3420
Website: http://www.advocatesforyouth.org
Advocates for Youth pushes a more positive and
    realistic approach to adolescent sexual and
    reproductive health.

Partnership for Prevention
1015 18th Street NW, Suite 300
Washington, DC 20036
(202) 833-0009
E-mail: info@prevent.org
This umbrella organization hopes to curb the
    spread of disease and promote preventative
    health practices.

Planned Parenthood
434 West 33rd Street
New York, NY 10001
(800) 230-7526
Website: http://www.plannedparenthood.org
Planned Parenthood offers STD screening and
    counseling in many locations nationwide.

Public Health Agency of Canada
130 Colonnade Road
A.L. 6501H
Ottawa, ON K1A 0K9
Canada
(604) 666-2083

Website: http://www.phac-aspc.gc.ca
This governmental agency promotes and pro-
    tects Canadians' health.

The Sex Information and Education Council of
    Canada
850 Coxwell Avenue
Toronto, ON M4C 5R1
Canada
Website: http://www.sieccan.org
SIECCAN runs public knowledge campaigns on
    sexual health and sexuality, especially in Can-
    ada's public schools.

U.S. Centers for Disease Control and Prevention
1600 Clifton Road
Atlanta, GA 30333
(800) 232-4636
Website: http://www.cdc.gov
The CDC leads federal efforts to prevent the
    spread of diseases, both at home and abroad.

WEBSITES

Because of the changing nature of Internet
links, Rosen Publishing has developed an online
list of websites related to the subject of this
book. This site is updated regularly. Please use
this link to access the list:

http://www.rosenlinks.com/YSH/Syph

FOR FURTHER READING

Allman, Tony. *Infectious Disease Research*. San Diego, CA: Referencepoint Press, 2011.

Cartwright, Frederick F., and Michael Biddiss. *Disease & History*. London, UK: Thistle Publishing, 2014.

Collins, Nicholas, and Samuel G. Woods. *Frequently Asked Questions About STDs*. New York, NY: Rosen Publishing, 2011.

Dougherty, Terri. *Sexually Transmitted Diseases*. Farmington Hills, MI: Lucent Books, 2010.

Feinstein, Stephen. *Sexuality and Teens: What You Should Know About Sex, Abstinence, Birth Control, Pregnancy and STDs*. New York, NY: Enslow Publishers, 2009.

McDowell, Josh. *The Bare Facts: 39 Questions Your Parents Hope You Never Ask About Sex*. Chicago, IL: Moody Publishers, 2011.

Reverby, Susan M. *Examining Tuskegee: The Infamous Syphilis Study and Its Legacy*. Chapel Hill, NC: The University of North Carolina Press, 2009.

Rogers, Kara, ed. *Infectious Diseases*. New York, NY: Rosen Publishing, 2011.

Schmaefsky, Brian, and David L. Heymann. *Syphilis*. New York, NY: Chelsea House, 2010.

Vincent, Beverly, and Robert Greenberger. *Frequently Asked Questions About Birth Control*. New York, NY: Rosen Publishing, 2011.

Wolny, Philip. *I Have an STD. Now What?* New York, NY: Rosen Publishing, 2015.

Yancey, Diane. *STDs*. Minneapolis, MN: Twenty-First Century Books, 2011.

BIBLIOGRAPHY

CDC.gov. "Male Latex Condoms and Sexually Transmitted Diseases." July 22, 2014. Retrieved October 10, 2014 (http://www.cdc.gov/condomeffectiveness/latex.htm).

CDC.gov. "Syphilis—CDC Fact Sheet." July 8, 2014. Retrieved October 10, 2014 (http://www.cdc.gov/std/syphilis/stdfact-syphilis.htm).

CDC.gov. "Syphilis: Detailed." Retrieved October 10, 2014 (http://www.cdc.gov/std/syphilis/STDFact-Syphilis-detailed.htm).

Crane, Misti. "Syphilis in Newborns Increasing." *Columbus Dispatch*, October 6, 2014. Retrieved October 10, 2014 (http://www.dispatch.com/content/stories/local/2014/10/06/syphilis-in-newborns-increasing.html).

Dotinga, Randy. "Death Knell for Syphilis?" *HealthDay News*, November 28, 2001. Retrieved October 10, 2014 (http://consumer.healthday.com/sexual-health-information-32/sex-health-news-603/death-knell-for-syphilis-404964.html).

Frith, John. "Syphilis—Its Early History and Treatment Until Penicillin and the Debate on Its Origins." *Journal of Military and Veterans' Health.* Retrieved October 10, 2014 (http://jmvh.org/article/syphilis-its-early-history-and-treatment-until-penicillin-and-the-debate-on-its-origins).

Haiken, Melanie. "Syphilis Made a Big Comeback in 2013, CDC Warns." Forbes.com, May

8, 2014. Retrieved October 10, 2014 (http://www.forbes.com/sites/melaniehaiken/2014/05/08/syphilis-making-a-big-comeback-among-men-warns-the-cdc).

Hayden, Deborah. *Pox: Genius, Madness, and the Mysteries of Syphilis.* New York, NY: Basic Books, 2003.

Mayo Clinic. "Diseases and Conditions: Syphilis." Retrieved October 13, 2014 (http://www.mayoclinic.org/diseases-conditions/syphilis/basics/definition/con-20021862).

McGreal, Chris. "Teen Pregnancy and Disease Rates Rose Sharply During Bush Years, Agency Finds." *Guardian*, July 20, 2009. Retrieved October 10, 2014 (http://www.theguardian.com/world/2009/jul/20/bush-teen-pregnancy-cdc-report).

Rodriguez, Diana. "Syphilis: A Highly Contagious, Stealthy Infection." Everydayhealth.com. Retrieved October 10, 2014 (http://www.everydayhealth.com/sexual-health/syphilis.aspx).

Rose, Mark. "Origins of Syphilis." *Archaeology*, January/February 1997. Retrieved October 10, 2014 (http://archive.archaeology.org/9701/newsbriefs/syphilis.html).

Science Daily. "Women Who Binge Drink at Greater Risk of Unsafe Sex and Sexually Transmitted Disease." September 15, 2008. Retrieved October 2014 (http://www.sciencedaily.com/releases/2008/09/080904215613.htm).

Tuohy, Lynne. "Al Capone Auction Documents Reveal Dementia, Violent Outbursts." *Huffington Post*, July 31, 2013. Retrieved October 10, 2014 (http://www.huffingtonpost.com/2013/05/31/al-capone-auction_n_3367770.html).

World Health Organization. "Over a Million Pregnant Women Infected with Syphilis Worldwide." Retrieved October 10, 2014 (http://www.who.int/reproductivehealth/topics/rtis/syphilis/pregnancy/en).

Wright, Katherine. "Where Did Syphilis Come From?" *Guardian*, October 26, 2013. Retrieved October 12, 2014 (http://www.theguardian.com/science/2013/oct/27/wellcome-prize-katherine-wright-syphilis-columbus).

INDEX

ABOUT THE AUTHOR

Philip Wolny is a writer from Queens, New York. His other teen wellness–related titles for Rosen Publishing include *I Have an STD. Now What?*, *The Truth About Heroin*, and *Abusing Prescription Drugs*.

PHOTO CREDITS